W9-ASB-856

CONTENTS

LAKE CLASSICS

*Great British and Irish
Short Stories I*

Rudyard
KIPLING

**Stories retold by Joanne Suter
Illustrated by James McConnell**

LAKE EDUCATION
Belmont, California

LAKE CLASSICS

Great American Short Stories I

Washington Irving, Nathaniel Hawthorne, Mark Twain, Bret Harte, Edgar Allan Poe, Kate Chopin, Willa Cather, Sarah Orne Jewett, Sherwood Anderson, Charles W. Chesnutt

Great American Short Stories II

Herman Melville, Stephen Crane, Ambrose Bierce, Jack London, Edith Wharton, Charlotte Perkins Gilman, Frank R. Stockton, Hamlin Garland, O. Henry, Richard Harding Davis

Great British and Irish Short Stories I

Arthur Conan Doyle, Saki (H. H. Munro), Rudyard Kipling, Katherine Mansfield, Thomas Hardy, E. M. Forster, Robert Louis Stevenson, H. G. Wells, John Galsworthy, James Joyce

Great Short Stories from Around the World I

Guy de Maupassant, Anton Chekhov, Leo Tolstoy, Selma Lagerlöf, Alphonse Daudet, Mori Ogwai, Leopoldo Alas, Rabindranath Tagore, Fyodor Dostoevsky, Honoré de Balzac

Cover and Text Designer: Diann Abbott

Library of Congress Catalog Number: 94-075353
ISBN 1-56103-028-7
Printed in the United States of America
1 9 8 7 6 5 4 3 2

❧ Lake Classic Short Stories ❧

> *"The universe is made of stories, not atoms."*
> —Muriel Rukeyser

> *"The story's about you."*
> —Horace

Everyone loves a good story. It is hard to think of a friendlier introduction to classic literature. For one thing, short stories are *short*—quick to get into and easy to finish. Of all the literary forms, the short story is the least intimidating and the most approachable.

Great literature is an important part of our human heritage. In the belief that this heritage belongs to everyone, *Lake Classic Short Stories* are adapted for today's readers. Lengthy sentences and paragraphs are shortened. Archaic words are replaced. Modern punctuation and spellings are used. Many of the longer stories are abridged. In all the stories, painstaking care has been taken to preserve the author's unique voice.

Lake Classic Short Stories have something for everyone. The hundreds of stories in the collection cover a broad terrain of themes, story types, and styles. Literary merit was a deciding factor in story selection. But no story was included unless it was as enjoyable as it was instructive. And special priority was given to stories that shine light on the human condition.

Each book in the *Lake Classic Short Stories* is devoted to the work of a single author. Little-known stories of merit are included with famous old favorites. Taken as a whole, the collected authors and stories make up a rich and diverse sampler of the story-teller's art.

Lake Classic Short Stories guarantee a great reading experience. Readers who look for common interests, concerns, and experiences are sure to find them. Readers who bring their own gifts of perception and appreciation to the stories will be doubly rewarded.

❦ Rudyard Kipling ❦
(1865–1936)

About the Author

Rudyard Kipling, the son of English parents, was born in Bombay, India. His father was in the service of the British government. When he was six, young Rudyard was taken home to England. There he was left to be raised by paid foster parents.

Kipling returned to India at the age of 17. There he was struck by the exotic qualities of Indian and military life. It was then that he began writing the colorful stories and poems that would later make him famous.

By the time he was 21, Kipling had written many short stories. The famous tale, "The Man Who Would Be King," is a story of greed and ambition in India.

Kipling suffered from very poor eyesight. A good friend of his, E. Kay

Robinson, remembered that Kipling was forever cleaning his thick glasses. Why? "Kipling was always laughing," Robinson said. "When you laugh till you nearly cry, your spectacles get misty." He said he would never forget the sight of Kipling, "shaking all over with laughter—and wiping his spectacles at the same time with his handkerchief."

Kipling's first novel, *The Light That Failed*, was about advancing blindness. The theme of this story was no doubt inspired by his own poor eyesight. His popular books for children were written during a four-year stay in the United States. Even today young people enjoy reading The *Jungle Book*, *Kim*, *Just So Stories*, and *Captains Courageous*.

In 1907, Kipling became the first Englishman to win the Nobel Prize.

If you like stories with exotic, foreign settings and colorful characters, you'll enjoy reading Kipling.

The Phantom Rickshaw

What can you do when a mistake keeps coming back to haunt you? In this suspenseful story, a man tries to get free of an old romance. But how can he marry Kitty if Agnes won't let him go?

THE RICKSHAW HOOD HAD FALLEN BACK. INSIDE SAT
MRS. WESSINGTON, HER GOLDEN HEAD BOWED LOW.

The Phantom Rickshaw

May no ill dreams disturb my rest
Nor Powers of Darkness me molest.
                              Evening Hymn

There are not many ways in which India is better than England. But one is that, in India, people get to know each other well. After five years of government service, a man knows—or at least knows something about—all of the 200 or 300 Englishmen in his province. In 10 years he should know twice as many people. At the end of 20 years, he should know something about every Englishman in the Empire. In fact, he may travel anywhere and everywhere without paying hotel bills. All houses are open to him. This small world is very, very kind and helpful. Let me give you an example.

A man named Rickett, from Kamartha, stayed with a man named Polder, in Kumaon, some 15 or so years ago. He meant to stay two nights, but he fell ill. For six weeks he stayed at Polder's house. In fact, he nearly died in Polder's bedroom. Before he finally left, Rickett caused a good deal of trouble for Polder's household.

From that time on, Polder looked upon Rickett as his responsibility. Each year he sent Rickett's family a box of presents. This is how it is. Even people who do not like you will stand by you. They will work themselves to the bone for you if you fall sick or into serious trouble.

Heatherlegh is a kindly English doctor working in India. He gives the same kind advice to all his patients. *"Lie low, go slow, and keep cool,"* is what he says. Dr. Heatherlegh believes that most men are killed by overwork. He says that it was overwork that killed Mr. Pansay. Pansay died in his care about three years ago. Heatherlegh laughs at my idea that there was a crack in Pansay's head. But I say that a little bit of the Dark World came through that crack and pressed him to death.

"Pansay simply went off the handle," says Dr. Heatherlegh. "He may or may not have behaved badly toward Mrs. Wessington. But I believe that overwork got him down. He made too much of an ordinary romance. He certainly was engaged to Miss Mannering, and she certainly broke the engagement. Then he caught a fever and all that nonsense about ghosts began. But it was overwork that started his illness. In the end it killed him, poor devil. But it was all caused by a system that asks one man to do the work of two and a half men."

I do not believe this. I used to sit up with Pansay sometimes. The man would describe in a low, even voice the parade that was always passing at the foot of his bed.

I suggested that he should write out everything he saw, from beginning to end. My idea was that it might ease his mind to put his fears in writing. He had a high fever while he was writing. And— sad to say—the words he wrote did not calm him.

But even when he was said to be fit enough to return to work, he did not. Pansay seemed to *want* to die. At the last he said that the woman still haunted him. I got his writings before he died.

This is his story, dated 1885, exactly as he wrote it:

My doctor tells me that I need rest and a change of air. I shall probably get both before long. I shall have a rest from which nothing can wake me—and a change of air far beyond this world. In the meantime, I plan to stay where I am. Against my doctor's orders, I will tell the world what has happened to me. You shall learn for yourselves exactly what has caused my illness. Then you may decide for yourselves whether any man on this earth was ever in more pain than I am right now.

I am speaking to you now like a man sentenced to death. You must listen to my story, wild as it is. But I am sure you will not believe it. Two months ago, I would have called anyone with such a tale either mad or drunk. But two months ago I was the happiest man in India. Today there is no one more miserable.

My doctor and I are the only two who know this. He explains that my brain, stomach, and eyes are all slightly sick. This, he says, makes me imagine things. *Imagine?* Indeed, I call him a fool. But you shall decide for yourselves.

Three years ago it was my luck—my bad luck—to sail to Bombay after a holiday. On board my ship was a woman named Agnes Wessington. She was the wife of an army officer. Before the trip had ended, both she and I were completely, madly in love with one another.

In matters of the heart, there is always one who gives love and another who takes it. From the first day of our meeting, I saw that Agnes's love was stronger than mine. Whether she saw that then, I do not know. Afterwards it was very plain to both of us.

Our ship arrived in Bombay in the spring of the year. We went our own ways and met no more for the next three or four months. Then my business took me to Simla. Her love led her to follow me there. We spent the season in Simla together. There the fire of my love burnt to an end with the closing year.

I neither make excuses nor say I'm sorry for that. It is true that Mrs. Wessington had given up much for me. She was prepared to give up everything. But in August of 1882, I told her that I was tired of her company and tired of the sound of her voice.

Now, 99 women out of 100 would have tired of me as I tired of them. And 75 out of 100 would have gotten even with me by turning their attentions to other men. Mrs. Wessington was the 100th, who did neither. I made clear my wish to stop seeing her. I was, in fact, quite cruel about it. But nothing I did stopped her attentions.

"Jack, darling!" was her constant cry. "I'm sure it's all a mistake, a terrible mistake. We'll be good friends again some day. *Please* forgive me, Jack, dear."

Forgive *her*? I was the one who had done wrong. I knew it. But my feelings for her had turned from pity to boredom to blind hate. And with this hate in my heart, the season of 1882 came to an end.

The next year we met again at Simla. Again she wore her same sad face. She made her same poor tries at getting together with me again. And I felt the same hate for her in every bone in my body. Several times I could not help but meet her alone. On each meeting her words were exactly the same. There was still her silly cry that it was all a "mistake." There was still her wish that we might again become "friends."

I might have seen what was happening, had I cared enough to look closely. I might have realized that it was only hope that was keeping her alive. She was growing more pale and thin with every month. Surely you will agree that her actions would have driven anyone to anger. It was uncalled for. It was childish. I believe that she was much to blame.

And yet, sometimes in the black nights when I'm filled with fever, I wonder about it. Then I begin to think that I might have been a little kinder to her. But what could I have done? I could not have gone on pretending to love her when I didn't—could I? It would have been unfair to us both.

Last year we met again. It was the same as before. There were her same old cries and the same short answers. I tried to make her see that we would never be together again. And as the season wore on, we saw less of each other.

When I think it over quietly in my sickroom, the season of 1884 seems like a bad dream. Somehow it is filled with both light and darkness.

I remember my outings with little Kitty Mannering. I think of our long rides on horseback together, when I talked of my love for her. I can again hear her sweet answers.

But now and again a yellow rickshaw would drive by. The four fellows who pulled the carriage were dressed in black and white. And inside that carriage I would catch sight of a white face—and the wave of Mrs. Wessington's hand.

I loved Kitty Mannering. I honestly loved her. And my love for her grew along with my hatred for Agnes Wessington. In August, Kitty and I were engaged to be married. The next day I met Mrs. Wessington's rickshaw in a back street. I felt a bit sorry for her, so I stopped to tell her everything. But she knew it already.

"So, I hear you're engaged, Jack dear!" she greeted me. "I'm sure it's all a mistake, a terrible mistake. You'll see! One day we shall be as good friends as we ever were."

I can see now that I was cruel to her. My answer might have hurt even a strong man. It cut the dying woman before me like the blow of a whip.

"Please forgive me, Jack," she cried. "I didn't mean to make you angry. But it's true, it's true!"

Then Mrs. Wessington broke down completely. I turned away and left her to finish my journey in peace. For just a moment or two, I felt like a mean dog. But when I looked back, I saw that she had turned her rickshaw. She had the idea, I suppose, of catching up with me.

The scene is like a picture in my mind. I can see the rain-swept sky, the dark, wet pines, the muddy road, and the black cliffs. Against this gloomy background stood out the black and white uniforms of the servants and the yellow rickshaw. Inside I could see Mrs. Wessington's bowed golden head. She was holding her handkerchief in her left hand and leaning back on the rickshaw pillows. I turned my horse up a path and ran away. Once I thought I heard someone crying "Jack!" but this may have been in my mind. I never looked back. Ten minutes later I came across Kitty riding on horseback. Just the thought of a long ride with her made me happy. I quickly forgot all about my meeting with the rickshaw.

A week later Mrs. Wessington became ill and died. It was as if a heavy load had been lifted from my life. I traveled about and was perfectly happy. Before three months were over, I had forgotten all about her. Only when I would come upon some of her old letters would I be reminded of the past. By January I had found all that was left of her letters and burnt them.

At the beginning of April of this year, 1885, I was back at Simla once more. Soon Kitty and I were deep in lover's talks and walks. We decided to be married at the end of June. Loving Kitty as I did, you will understand that I saw myself as the happiest man in India.

Some 14 wonderful days passed quickly. Then, on the 15th of April, I pointed out to Kitty that she should have a ring. We went straight to the jewelers to have one fitted for her. Remember— though my doctor may not agree—that I was then in perfect health. My mind and spirit were sound. Kitty and I entered the jewelry shop together and bought a ring with two diamonds. Then we rode out by the bridge.

While my horse was carefully feeling his way over the loose ground, Kitty was laughing and chattering at my side. The streets were crowded, but I soon became aware that someone far away was calling my name. It struck me that I had heard the voice before, but I could not remember when or where. At last I decided it must have been just a humming in my ears.

But then something strange caught my eye. It was four fellows in black and white uniforms pulling a yellow rickshaw. There's no way to describe the flood of bad memories this sight brought back to me. For a moment I thought of hiring the men myself and pulling the black and white coats from off their backs.

"Kitty," I cried, "there are poor Mrs. Wessington's men! I wonder who has hired them now?"

Kitty had known Mrs. Wessington slightly last season. She had always been interested in the sickly woman.

"What? Where?" she asked. "I can't see them anywhere."

Even as she spoke, her horse moved directly in front of the rickshaw. I had scarcely time to call out a word of warning. To my horror, horse and rider passed *through* the men and carriage as if they had been thin air!

"Why, what's the matter?" cried Kitty. "What made you call out so foolishly, Jack? If you think I can't ride....There!"

Kitty set off, her sweet little head in the air, at a hard gallop. She thought that I would follow her. What was the matter? Either I was mad or drunk—or Simla was haunted with devils. I pulled up my horse and turned around. The rickshaw had turned too. Now it stood facing me, near the railing of the bridge.

"Jack! Jack, darling!" (There was no mistake about the words this time. They rang through my head as if they had been shouted in my ear.) "It's some terrible mistake, I'm sure. *Please* forgive me, Jack. Let's be friends again."

The rickshaw hood had fallen back. Inside sat Mrs. Wessington. Her handkerchief was in hand, and her golden head was bowed low.

I stared. I don't know how long it was before I moved. Then I tumbled off my horse and ran. Half fainting, I stumbled into a cafe. There were two or three couples gathered around the coffee tables. Their talk made me feel better, so I joined them. Soon I was chatting and laughing. But my face, when I caught sight of it in a mirror, was as white as that of a dead man. Three or four men noticed my strange looks. I think they thought I'd had too much to drink. I must have talked for about ten minutes or so, though it seemed forever to me. Then I heard Kitty's clear voice outside. She was asking for me. In another minute, she entered the shop. I knew she would be angry with me for leaving her. But something in my face stopped her.

"Why, Jack," she cried. "What *have* you been doing? What has *happened*? Are you sick?" I had to lie. I said that the sun had been a little too much for me. But it was close to five o'clock on a cloudy April afternoon. The sun had been hidden all day. I saw my mistake as soon as the words were out of my mouth. I followed an angry Kitty out of the cafe. Then I climbed on my horse and rode away to my hotel, leaving Kitty to finish the ride by herself.

In my room I sat down and tried to think over the matter calmly. Here was I, Jack Pansay, a well-educated man in the year of 1885. I was sound of mind and body. Yet I'd been driven from my sweetheart's side by a ghost. A woman who had been dead and buried eight months ago was calling out to me. These were the facts.

When Kitty and I left the jewelry shop, nothing was farther from my mind than Mrs. Wessington. Nothing was unusual about the road we traveled. It was broad daylight. The streets were full of people. And yet there had appeared to me a face from the grave.

My first hope was that there might be some woman who looked just like Mrs. Wessington. Perhaps this woman had hired the same carriage and its men. But that hope was lost when Kitty's horse had gone *through* the rickshaw. Again and again I went over the scene in my mind. Again and again I gave up. I could not explain it.

I thought of telling Kitty all about it and of begging her to marry me at once. Together we would beat the ghostly rider in the rickshaw! Then I argued with myself. "Surely the sight of the rickshaw itself is enough to prove that it was not a ghost. Suppose I really *had* seen the ghost of a dead woman—but what about the men in black and white? The whole thing is silly! Imagine, the ghosts of all four men!"

Next morning I sent a note to Kitty. I told her I was sorry about my strange actions the day before. I explained that I had felt sick. Kitty believed my story. That afternoon we rode out with the shadow of my first lie between us.

Nothing would please her but a ride in the same places where I had often met Mrs. Wessington. I tried to suggest other roads, but she was still angry and a little hurt. So I gave in, and we set out together. First we rode slowly together, but then the horses picked up speed. My own heart beat quicker as we neared the top of a hill. All afternoon my mind had been full of Mrs. Wessington. Every inch of the road reminded me of our old-time walks and talks. The rocks were full of it. The pines sang it overhead. The rain-fed streams laughed over the story. The wind in my ears told the tale aloud.

Then, in the middle of the road, the Horror was waiting for me. No other rickshaw was in sight. Only the four men dressed in black and white, the yellow carriage, the golden head of the woman within. All were just as I had left them eight and a half months ago!

For a second I thought that Kitty *must* see what I saw. But her next words were, "Not a soul in sight! Come along, Jack, and I'll race you." Her horse shot ahead and mine followed close behind.

Half a minute brought us within 50 yards of the rickshaw. I slowed my horse and fell back a little. The rickshaw was right in the middle of the road! Once more, Kitty's horse passed right through it. My horse followed. "Jack! Jack dear! Please forgive me," rang the cry in my ears. "It's all been a mistake, a terrible mistake."

I dug my heels into my horse. But when I looked behind me, the rickshaw was still waiting, ever waiting, against the gray hillside. And the wind brought me the words again. Kitty teased me about my silence throughout the rest of the ride.

I was to dine with Kitty's family that night. There was just enough time for me to ride home to dress. On the road I heard two men talking together in the dusk. "It's a strange thing," said one, "how completely all signs of it disappeared.

You know, my wife was very fond of the woman. I never could see anything in the old girl myself. But my wife wanted me to buy her old rickshaw and her servants, too, if they were to be sold. The man she hired it from told me a strange story indeed. He said that all four of the servants—they were brothers—died of a fever, poor devils. He said he broke up the rickshaw himself. Told me he would never use a dead woman's rickshaw. It would spoil his luck. Strange idea, eh? Imagine poor little Mrs. Wessington spoiling anyone's luck except her own!"

Hearing these words, I laughed out loud. My own laugh surprised me. So there *were* ghosts of rickshaws after all! How much did Mrs. Wessington pay her servants in the other world? What were their hours? Where did they go?

Then, as if in answer to my last question, I saw the terrible Thing blocking my path in the twilight. The dead travel fast and by short cuts not known to others. I laughed out loud a second time. Then I held back my laughter, for I was afraid that I was going mad.

I remember that I stopped my horse at the head of the rickshaw. There I politely wished Mrs. Wessington a good evening. Her reply was one I knew only too well. I listened to the end. Then I answered that I had heard it all before and wondered if she had anything more to say. Some evil devil stronger than I must have entered into me that evening. I remember talking for five minutes to the Thing in front of me.

"Mad as a hatter, poor devil, or drunk. Max, try to get him to come home."

Surely *that* was not Mrs. Wessington's voice! No. The two men on the road had heard me speaking to the empty air. They had returned to look after me. They seemed to think I was very drunk, and they were very kind. I thanked them and rode away to my hotel. There I changed clothes and arrived at the Mannerings' ten minutes late.

At dinner I was talking quietly to my sweetheart. Suddenly I noticed a short, red-whiskered man at the far end of the table. He was telling about his meeting with a crazy man that evening.

A few sentences later, I knew that he was talking about me. He had seen what had happened only a half an hour ago. In the middle of the story he looked around. When he caught my eye, he stopped talking. After a long moment, the red-whiskered man said that he had "forgotten the rest." I silently thanked him from the bottom of my heart and went on eating my fish.

At last, that dinner came to an end. I left Kitty, knowing as surely as I lived that It would be waiting for me outside the door. The red-whiskered man, who had been introduced to me as Dr. Heatherlegh of Simla, stopped me. He offered to keep me company on the road. I thanked him.

My fears were real. The rickshaw lay waiting in the street with its head-lamp lighted. The red-whiskered man got right to the point.

"I say, Pansay—what in the world was the matter with you when we met earlier?" I answered before I had time to think.

"That!" said I, pointing to It.

"*That* may only mean that you are drunk, or that you have bad eyes. Now you don't drink much. I saw that at dinner. So you can't be drunk. There is nothing whatever where you are pointing. But you're shaking like a scared pony. Therefore, it must be bad eyes. Come along home with me."

Instead of waiting for us, the rickshaw kept about 20 yards ahead. In the course of that long night ride, I told the doctor almost as much as I have told you here.

"Come home and do what I tell you, young man," said he. "I'll make you well. But let this be a lesson to you! Steer clear of women and heavy food until the day of your death."

The rickshaw stayed right in front of us. My red-whiskered friend seemed to enjoy hearing exactly where it was.

"Eyes, Pansay. Eyes, brain, and stomach. Your brain is too selfish, your stomach is too weak, and your eyes are strained. What you need is a liver pill. I'll take complete medical charge of you from this hour on! You are far too interesting a case to be passed over."

Just then the rickshaw came to a dead stop under an overhanging cliff. I stopped too, explaining my reason.

Heatherlegh wanted to go forward. Then suddenly he cried, "Lord, have mercy! What's that?"

There was a loud noise and a blinding cloud of dust just in front of us. Then about ten yards of cliffside slid down into the road below! Our two horses stood still, sweating with fear. Finally, the rattle of falling earth and stone stopped. The doctor whispered, "Man, if we had gone forward, we would have been ten feet deep in our graves by now. Come home, Pansay, and thank God."

We took another road and arrived at Dr. Heatherlegh's house just after midnight. He began working on my cure right away. For a week I never left his sight. Many times that week I thanked the good luck which had thrown me together with Heatherlegh. He was Simla's best and kindest doctor.

Day by day my spirits grew lighter. And day by day, I became more willing to believe Heatherlegh's eyes, brain, and stomach idea.

I wrote to Kitty, explaining that I had hurt my ankle in a fall from my horse. This, I wrote, had kept me indoors for a few days. I promised that she would see me soon.

Heatherlegh's plan was simple. There were liver pills, cold-water baths, and strong exercise.

At the end of the week, he looked me over. He gave me even stricter rules about food and exercise. Then, as quickly as he had taken charge of me, Heatherlegh told me to go. These were his words of good-bye: "Man, your mind is well, as is your body. Now, get your things out of this house as soon as you can. Be off to Miss Kitty."

I tried to put my thanks into words, but he cut me short.

"Don't think I did this because I like you. I see that you have acted rather badly in the past. But, all the same, you are such an unusual case. No!" he said, pushing back my hand. "No payment, please. In fact, I'll pay *you* if you ever see that thing again!"

Half an hour later I was in the Mannerings' drawing room with Kitty. I felt drunk with happiness. Somehow I knew that I should never again be troubled by the horrible, ghostly rickshaw. I was so sure of this that I asked Kitty to go out for a ride with me.

Never had I been so full of energy and good spirits! Never had I been so happy as I was on the afternoon of April 30th. Kitty was pleased with the change in my mood. We left the Mannerings' house together, laughing and talking.

I was in a hurry to ride about and prove that It was gone. The horses seemed all too slow to me that day. Kitty was surprised by my high spirits. "Why, Jack!" she cried, "you are acting like a child. What are you doing?"

"Doing?" I answered. "Nothing, dear. That's just it. If you'd been doing nothing for a week except lying in bed, you'd be as spirited as I."

The words were hardly out of my lips before we rounded the next corner. There, in the center of the road, stood the yellow rickshaw and Mrs. Wessington. I pulled up my horse. I stared and then rubbed my eyes. Then, I believe, I must have said something. The next thing I knew was that I was lying face down on the road. Kitty was kneeling above me in tears.

"Has it gone, child?" I gasped. Kitty only cried harder.

"Has *what* gone, Jack dear? What does all this mean? There must be a mistake somewhere, Jack. A terrible mistake!" Her last words brought me to my feet. I was shouting like a mad man.

"Yes, there *is* a mistake somewhere," I repeated, "a terrible mistake. Come and look at It."

I remember that I dragged Kitty by the arm along the road to where It stood. I begged her to speak to It. I asked her to tell It that we were going to be married—and that neither Death nor Hell could break the tie between us. In terror, I told the rickshaw that this was killing me. As I talked on, I suppose I must have told Kitty the whole story about me and Mrs. Wessington. I saw her face go white and her eyes blaze.

"Thank you, Mr. Pansay," she said. "That's *quite* enough."

As Kitty sprang into her saddle, I tried to hold her back. I begged her to hear me out and forgive me. My answer was the cut of her riding whip across my face from mouth to eye. Then she added a word or two of good-bye that even now I cannot write down. At last Kitty knew the whole story.

I staggered back to the side of the rickshaw. My face was cut and bleeding. The blow of the riding whip had raised a bright blue mark on my cheek. I had no self-respect left at all. Just then Dr. Heatherlegh, who must have been following Kitty and me, rode up.

"Doctor," I said, pointing to my face, "here is Miss Mannering's good-bye to me. I'll take that payment now."

The look on Heatherlegh's face, even in my great sorrow, moved me to laughter.

"I was so certain—" he began.

"Don't be a fool," I whispered. "I've lost my life's happiness. You'd better take me home."

As I spoke those words, the rickshaw was gone. I don't remember what happened next. The road seemed to roll like a wave, and darkness fell upon me.

Seven days later, on the 7th of May, I awoke to find that I was lying in Heatherlegh's room. I felt as weak as a little child. Heatherlegh was watching me from behind the papers on his writing table. His first words were not welcome ones, but I was too tired to care.

"Here are your letters. Miss Kitty has returned them all. And here's a package that looks like a ring. It came with a note from Kitty's father. The old gentleman is not pleased with you."

"And Kitty?" I asked quietly.

"You must have told her some dark secrets before I caught up with you. She writes that a man who would have treated a woman as you did Mrs. Wessington ought to kill himself. She's a hot-headed girl. She says she'll die before she ever speaks to you again."

I groaned and turned on my other side.

"Now you have your choice, my friend. This engagement has to be broken off.

The Mannerings don't want to be too hard on you. Shall we say your engagement was broken because you are a drunk—or because you have fits?

"Sorry I can't offer you a better reason. Unless you'd prefer I say you are crazy. Just say the word, and I'll tell them it's fits. By now the whole town knows about the scene you made in the street. Come! I'll give you five minutes to think it over."

During those five minutes, I felt as if I were crawling through the darkest pit. All my choices were bad ones. Then I heard myself answering in a voice I hardly knew as my own.

"Tell them I have fits, Heatherlegh. And send them my love. Now let me sleep a bit longer."

For hours I tossed and turned in my bed. Step by step, I went over and over all that had happened in the past month.

"But I am in Simla," I kept saying to myself. "I, Jack Pansay, am in Simla.

There are no ghosts here. Why couldn't Agnes have left me alone? I never did her any harm. Suppose *she* had been the one to leave me broken hearted? I'd never have come back on purpose to kill *her*! Why can't I be left alone—left alone and happy?"

It was high noon when I first awoke. But the sun was low in the sky before I slept—too worn to feel further pain.

The next day I could not leave my bed. In the morning Dr. Heatherlegh told me that an answer had come from Mr. Mannering. The story of my illness had passed through the whole of Simla. Everyone felt sorry for me.

"And that's rather more than you deserve," he ended pleasantly. "But, heaven knows, you have had a pretty tough time. Never mind! We will cure you yet, you strange man."

I shook my head. "You've been much too good to me already, old man," said I.

"But I must not trouble you further."

In my heart I knew that nothing Heatherlegh could do would help me. I felt a sense of hopeless anger against it all. After all, there were thousands of men no better than I. *Their* punishments would at least wait until after their deaths!

I felt it was not fair that I alone should have been singled out for so terrible a fate.

Then suddenly it seemed to me that the rickshaw and I were the only real things in this world. It seemed that Kitty was a ghost. It seemed that Mannering, Heatherlegh, and the other men and women I knew were all ghosts.

I tossed and turned for seven days. My body grew stronger and stronger. At last the bedroom mirror told me that I looked like other men again. I could return to everyday life. It was strange that my face showed no signs of the struggle I had gone through. It was pale, yes—but there was no look of horror. It was odd that I should see no sign of the sickness that was eating me away. Yet I found nothing.

On the 15th of May, I left Dr. Heatherlegh's house. It was eleven o'clock in the morning. I drove to the Club. There I found that every man knew my story as told by Heatherlegh. Each was very kind. But I saw something else very clearly. For the rest of my life, I would be set apart from my friends.

I ate lunch at the Club and then wandered down the streets in hope of meeting Kitty. It was not long before the yellow rickshaw joined me. I heard Mrs. Wessington's voice at my side.

I had been waiting for this ever since I came out. My only surprise was that it had taken her so long. In silence, the phantom rickshaw and I went side by side along the road.

Close to the shops, Kitty and a man

on horseback rode by us. For any sign she gave, I might have been a dog in the road. So Kitty and her friend—and I and my ghostly love—rode through the streets in couples. The road was streaming with water. The air was full of a fine, driving rain.

Two or three times, I said to myself, "I'm Jack Pansay of Simla! Everyday, ordinary Simla! I must not forget that. I must not forget that." Then I would try to remember some talk I heard at the Club, or the price of someone's horse, or anything that was ordinary and common place. I even repeated the multiplication tables quickly to myself—to make sure I was not going mad. It seemed to make me feel better. And, for a time, it kept me from hearing Mrs. Wessington's voice.

When Kitty and the man broke into a gallop, I was left alone with Mrs. Wessington. "Agnes," said I, "will you put back your hood and tell me what it all means?" The hood dropped silently. *I was face to face with my dead and buried lover.* She was wearing the dress in which I had last seen her alive. She carried the same tiny handkerchief in her right hand and the same case of calling cards in her left. I quickly repeated the multiplication tables to steady myself.

"Agnes," I said again. "Please tell me what it all means." Mrs. Wessington leaned forward. She gave that odd, quick turn of the head I used to know so well. Then she spoke.

My story has already been hard to accept. I know that no one—not even Kitty, for whom I have written it all down—will ever believe me. But I must finish telling it for my own sake.

Mrs. Wessington spoke, and I walked with her as I might walk by the side of any living woman's rickshaw. I seemed to move in a world of ghosts. We two joined the crowd of people in the streets. As I saw them, it seemed that *they* were the shadows that divided for the rickshaw to pass through.

What we said during the course of that strange talk, I cannot—indeed, I dare not—tell. It was terrible. Yet, in some way that is hard to describe, it was a wonderful moment. Could it be possible? Was I meant to win—for a second time—the woman I had killed by my own cruelty?

I met Kitty on the homeward road. She was just a shadow among shadows.

I cannot describe all that happened during the next two weeks. My story would never come to an end, and you would grow tired of it. But morning after morning and evening after evening, the ghostly rickshaw and I wandered through Simla together. Wherever I went, the four servants in black and white went with me. I found them outside the theater and outside the Club. They waited for me to appear, even in broad daylight when I went calling.

The rickshaw looked real in every way except that it cast no shadow. More than once I had to stop myself from warning someone against riding right into it. More than once I have walked down the streets, deep in conversation with Mrs. Wessington, to the surprise of all who passed me by.

Soon I learned that people no longer believed the "fits" story. They called me a mad man. But I made no change in my life. I called on friends. I rode about as freely as ever. I wanted to be with people all the time. I hungered to be in the real world. Yet, at the same time, I felt rather unhappy when I had been away too long from my ghostly lady. It would be almost impossible to describe my moods from the 15th of May until today.

The sight of the rickshaw filled me with different feelings. Sometimes I would feel horror and blind fear. And sometimes I would feel a strange sort of pleasure. I dared not leave Simla. Yet I knew that my stay there was killing me. I knew, indeed, that I was meant to die slowly and a little bit every day.

I watched for Kitty. But I did not mind seeing her go out with other men. She was as much out of my life as I was out of hers. By day I wandered with Mrs. Wessington—almost happily. By night I begged Heaven to let me return to the life I used to know. And always I felt a dull wonder that the Seen and the Unseen should come together on this earth to chase one poor soul to its grave.

* * * *

August 27. Heatherlegh has not left my side. Only yesterday he told me I should ask for sick leave. Imagine—sick leave to escape a ghost! Imagine getting rid of five ghosts and a phantom rickshaw by going away to England! Heatherlegh's idea made me laugh wildly. I told him that I would wait quietly for the end at Simla. And I am sure that the end is not far off. Believe me, it frightens me more than any words can say. Each night I wonder just exactly how I shall die.

Shall I die in my bed peacefully, as an English gentleman should die? Or, in one last walk on the streets, will my soul be grabbed from me? Will it take its place forever by the side of that ghostly terror? Shall I love Agnes again in the next world? Or shall I hate her and yet be tied to her side forever? As the day draws nearer, I fear the spirits from beyond the grave more and more.

It is an awful thing to die with not one-half of your life completed. It is even more awful to wait for the end without knowing what it will be. Pity me—at least for what you might call madness! I know you will never believe what I have written here. Yet as surely as a man was ever killed by the Powers of Darkness, I am that man.

Be fair, too, and pity her. For as surely as ever a woman was killed by a man—I killed Mrs. Wessington. And the last part of my punishment is even now upon me.

A Bank Fraud

Is a gentleman a gentleman in *all* circumstances? In this story, an unpleasant new accountant comes to work at the bank. How can Reggie be so patient with his constant complaining?

THE DIRECTORS HAD SENT REGGIE A NEW ACCOUNTANT
FROM ENGLAND.

A Bank Fraud

He drank strong waters and
his speech was coarse;
He purchased clothing but
forgot to pay;
He stuck a trusting young man
with a horse,
And won at games in a
doubtful way.
Then, between his vice and
folly, turned aside
To do good deeds and then to
hide them, lied.
                    —The Mess Room

If Reggie Burke were in India now, he would not want me to tell this tale. But since he is in Hong Kong and won't see it, it is safe to tell. He was the man who worked the big fraud on the Sind and Sialkote Bank.

Everybody liked Reggie. He was the manager of the bank's up-country branch. People knew that he was a sound businessman with good, solid banking experience. And he also knew how to combine the pleasures of everyday life with his work. He did very well at both. Reggie Burke could ride any horse there was—and he danced as nicely as he rode. He was invited to every party.

He always said that there were two Reggie Burkes. Between four in the afternoon and ten, there was "Reggie Burke, ready for anything from games to riding to picnics." Between ten in the morning and four, there was "Mr.

Reginald Burke, Manager of the Sind and Sialkote Branch Bank." You might play polo with him one afternoon, and the next morning you might call on him to take out a loan. He would recognize you, of course. But you would have some trouble recognizing him.

The bank had its head office in Calcutta. The directors of the bank picked their men carefully. They had tested Reggie, and he had satisfied them. They trusted him as much as directors ever trust managers. You must decide for yourself whether he deserved their trust.

Reggie's branch had a usual staff. There was one manager and one accountant. Both were English. There was also a cashier and a few native clerks. The police patrol came round at nights outside. It was a busy bank in a rich district.

Reggie, a clever man, made sure he

knew about the affairs of everyone in the area. Reggie was young-looking, clean-shaved, and he had a twinkle in his eye. He knew what he was doing.

One day, at a big dinner, he announced that the directors had sent him a new accountant from England. He called the man a "Natural Curiosity." He was right. Mr. Silas Riley, Accountant, was a most curious animal. He was a tall, thin fellow from a wealthy family. Silas Riley thought very highly of himself, to say the least. He had worked himself up, after seven years, to a cashier's position in the bank.

But Riley was new to the country. He had no idea that banking in India was so different from banking in England. He thought the directors had chosen him for this job because of his brilliant mind. He believed that they had great plans for him and his special talents. Also, Riley was sickly. He had some sort of trouble in his chest. This made him very short of temper.

You can see why Reggie called his new accountant a Natural Curiosity. The two men did not hit it off at all well. Riley thought that Reggie was a wild, feather-headed fool who spent too much time on fun. He saw Reggie as totally wrong for the serious job of banking. He could never get over Reggie's young looks and his "to-heck-with-you" air.

And Riley couldn't understand Reggie's friends. They were big, careless army men who came riding over to Sunday breakfasts at the bank. They often told off-color stories until Riley got up and left the room.

Riley was always telling Reggie how business should be handled. More than once, Reggie had to remind him that it was he—not Riley—who managed the bank. Then Riley got angry. He reminded Reggie that he was a dear friend of the directors. Reggie tore at his hair and shook his head at Riley's bragging. The trouble was that Reggie really needed Riley's help in the bank. It was a very busy branch.

In the winter, Riley fell sick with his lung problem. He was in bed for weeks. This threw more work on Reggie. But in some ways he didn't mind. It was better than the constant complaining that went on when Riley was well.

One of the traveling inspectors of the bank found out about Riley's illness. He reported this news to the directors, and they were not pleased. The fact was that Riley had moved up in the bank because one of the directors was a friend of Riley's father. But Riley's father had died. Now the directors began to wonder about an accountant who was sick for half the year. Hadn't he better give his place up to a healthy man?

If Riley had known how he came by his job, he might have behaved better. But he knew nothing. He was either sick at home, or he was at work, bothering Reggie in a hundred ways. In his mind, he was a great help to everyone. Reggie used to call him terrible names behind his back. But he never was cruel to his face. "Riley," he said, "is such a weak little beast. But half of his bad temper is due, no doubt, to the pains in his chest."

Late in April, Riley became very sick indeed. The doctor thumped his chest and told him he would be better before long. But then the doctor went to Reggie. "Do you know how sick your accountant is?" he asked.

"No!" said Reggie. "The worse the better—darn him! He's a pest when he is well. I'll give you all the money in the bank if you can keep him quiet through this hot weather!"

But the doctor did not laugh. "Man, I'm not joking," he said. "I'd say he only has about three more months to live. On my honor, that's all the time he has in this world. The sickness has hold of him to the bone."

Reggie's cheerful face changed at once into the serious face of "Mr. Reginald Burke." He asked, "What can I do?"

"Nothing," said the doctor. "For all purposes, the man is dead already. Just keep him quiet and cheerful. Tell him he's going to get well. That's all. I'll look after him to the end, of course."

Then the doctor went away, and Reggie sat down to open the evening mail. His first letter was one from the directors. They wrote that Mr. Riley was to leave his position. He should be given a month's notice. A letter to Riley himself would follow. Then the directors went on to tell Reggie about the new accountant who would be sent. He was a man Reggie knew and liked.

Reggie leaned back in his chair. He thought awhile. Soon, he found himself planning the fraud. He put away the directors' letter. Then he went in to talk to Riley. The sick man was as thankless and impossible as ever. He worried that the bank would not be able to get along without him during his illness. He never said a word about the extra work on Reggie's shoulders. He thought only of how his absence could hurt his own chances to move up in the bank.

Reggie told Riley that everything would be fine. He said that he would double check everything that happened at the bank. Riley calmed down a bit. But he hinted that he did not think much of Reggie's head for business. Reggie did

not say a word—even though the letter
in his desk could have silenced Riley in
a minute.

The days passed in the big darkened
house. The directors' letter to Riley
arrived saying that he was fired. Reggie
put the letter away. Every evening he
brought the account books from the bank
to Riley's room. He showed him all the
day's business, while Riley growled.
Reggie did his best to make things
pleasant for Riley. But no matter what
he did, the accountant was sure that the
bank was falling to ruin without him.

In June, the lying in bed began to get
Riley down. He asked whether his
absence had been noted by the directors.
Reggie said that they had written some
very nice letters. They hoped, Reggie
said, that he would be able to return to
his job before long. He showed Riley the
letters (which Reggie himself had
written). Riley said that he would prefer

A BANK FRAUD   69

it if Reggie did not open his mail. Reggie said he was sorry.

Then Riley's mood got even worse. He began to lecture Reggie on his evil ways and his bad friends. "Of course, lying here on my back, Mr. Burke, I can't keep a proper eye on you. But when I'm well, I *do* hope you'll take some note of my words."

Reggie had given up polo and dinners and tennis to care for Riley. But he never lost his temper. He simply said that he was sorry for all of Riley's complaints. And he promised to do better. Night after night, he settled Riley's head on a pillow and patiently listened. Night after night, he heard the warnings and complaints that now came in hard, dry whispers. He did this at the end of a heavy day's office work—doing the job of two men—in the latter half of June.

When the new accountant came, Reggie told him the facts of the case.

Then he told Riley that the new man was a guest who had come to visit. Riley said that he might have had better sense than to entertain his "wild friends" at such a time. So Reggie sent Carron, the new accountant, to a room at the Club.

Carron took some of the heavy work off Reggie's shoulders. This gave Reggie more time to spend at Riley's side. There he explained, calmed, settled and re-settled the poor man in his bed. He made up stories and wrote fake letters from the directors in Calcutta.

At the end of the first month, Riley wanted to send some money home to his mother. Reggie sent the money. At the end of the second month, Riley's salary was paid as usual. Reggie paid it out of his own pocket. Along with the money, he gave Riley a beautiful letter from the directors. Of course it was a letter Reggie had written himself.

By now Riley was very sick, indeed.

But still, the flame of his life burnt on. Now and then he would be cheerful and look brightly toward the future. He would talk of going home to England to see his mother. Reggie listened at the end of every busy day. He always nodded and agreed with the plans.

At other times, Riley wanted Reggie to read the Bible to him. Then he talked about Reggie's sins and how he must do better. He always found time to scold Reggie about the running of the bank. He never lost a chance to show Reggie where his weak points lay.

This indoor, sickroom life wore Reggie down a good deal. It shook his nerves and lowered his billiard play by 40 points. But the business of the bank—and the business of the sickroom—had to go on. Both jobs had to be done, even though the temperature was 116 degrees in the shade.

At the end of the third month, Riley

was sinking fast. He had begun to understand that he was very sick. "He needs something to care about if he is to hang on," said the doctor. "Keep him interested in life if you care about his staying alive."

So, though it made no sense at all, Reggie told Riley that he had received a 25-percent raise in salary from the directors. The lie worked beautifully. Riley was happy and cheerful. He was healthy in mind, though his body was weak. He lived on for a full month. Every day he growled and worried about the bank, and talked of the future. Every night he heard the Bible read, and lectured Reggie on sin.

But at the end of September, on a dreadfully hot evening, Riley suddenly rose up in bed. "Mr. Burke, I am going to die," he gasped. "I know it in myself. My chest is all hollow inside, and there's nothing to breathe with. I feel sure I have done nothing to be sorry for. God be thanked, I have not sinned. But I suggest that *you,* Mr. Burke . . ."

Then his voice died down. Reggie bent over him.

"Send my salary for September to my mother . . . done great things with the bank if I had lived . . . poor business practices . . . no fault of mine. . . ."

And he turned his face to the wall and died.

Reggie drew the sheet over his face and went out onto the porch. His last letter full of good words and cheer from the directors was unused in his pocket.

"If I'd been only ten minutes earlier with it," thought Reggie, "I might have pulled him through another day."

Thinking About
the Stories

The Phantom Rickshaw

1. All the events in a story are arranged in a certain order, or sequence. Tell about one event from the beginning of this story, one from the middle, and one from the end. How are these events related?

2. Look back at the illustration that introduces this story. What character or characters are pictured? What is happening in the scene? What clues does the picture give you about the time and place of the story?

3. In what town, city, or country does this story take place? Is the location important to the story? Why or why not?

A Bank Fraud

1. Good writing always has an effect on the reader. How did you feel when you finished reading this story? Were you surprised, horrified, amused, sad, touched, or inspired? What elements in the story made you feel that way?

2. What is the title of this story? Can you think of another good title?

3. Imagine that you have been asked to write a short review of this story. In one or two sentences, tell what the story is about and why someone would enjoy reading it.

Thinking About
the Book

1. Choose your favorite illustration in this book. Use this picture as a springboard to write a new story. Give the characters different names. Begin your story with something they are saying or thinking.

2. Compare the stories in this book. Which was the most interesting? Why? In what ways were they alike? In what ways different?

3. Good writers usually write about what they know best. If you wrote a story, what kind of characters would you create? What would be the setting?